What Happens When You Pray

Angel May

WESTBOW
PRESS®
A DIVISION OF THOMAS NELSON
& ZONDERVAN

Scripture quotations marked KJV are from the Holy Bible, King James
Version (Authorized Version). First published in 1611. Quoted from the KJV
Classic Reference Bible, Copyright 1983 by The Zondervan Corporation.

WestBow Press books may be ordered through booksellers or by contacting:

WestBow Press
A Division of Thomas Nelson & Zondervan
1663 Liberty Drive
Bloomington, IN 47403
www.westbowpress.com
1 (866) 928-1240

Because of the dynamic nature of the Internet, any web addresses or
links contained in this book may have changed since publication and
may no longer be valid. The views expressed in this work are solely those
of the author and do not necessarily reflect the views of the publisher,
and the publisher hereby disclaims any responsibility for them.

Any people depicted in stock imagery provided by Thinkstock are models,
and such images are being used for illustrative purposes only.
Certain stock imagery © Thinkstock.

ISBN: 978-1-5127-8409-1 (sc)
ISBN: 978-1-5127-8410-7 (hc)
ISBN: 978-1-5127-8408-4 (e)

Library of Congress Control Number: 2017906230

Print information available on the last page.

WestBow Press rev. date: 5/2/2017

"If my people, which are called by my name, shall humble themselves, and pray, and seek my face, and turn from their wicked ways; then will I hear from heaven, and will forgive their sin, and will heal their land."

—2 Chronicles 7:14, KJV

Contents

A Call to Pray

I wrote this book because there is a call in the Spirit to pray. I call you to fall on your knees and seek the face of God. What if something bad was about to happen in the world, in your city, or in your country—and you could prevent it by praying? What would you do? What if God was about to show up in your life, and good was coming your way—and all you had to do was pray?

God is about to do a new thing in your life, and you

shall know it (Isa. 43:19). Your life is about to change: your broken marriage will be put back together, or your prodigal son or daughter shall return home. You are about to hear from God. There will be deliverance in your house, from every evil in the name of Jesus! You are about to experience a move of God like you have never experienced before in your life. There is going to be a shift in the atmosphere. What you see today will be no more tomorrow. Your weeping will be turned to laughter. "Weeping may endure for a night but joy comes in the morning" *(Ps. 30:5).*

More and more young people will run off the streets and run into the house of the Lord; they shall be saved. God is about to answer your prayer. Do not give up on the brink of your miracle. Yes, a miracle is about to happen in your life. Glory to God! Dry your tears. It is not over until the final word comes from God. He is saying, "Do not give up on praying. Keep praying; pray and pray." I am living in a country chosen by a God of much blessings, wealth, and prosperity. You cannot allow the evil one access to undo everything that has been built by the great fathers and mothers who laid the precious foundation of America. The constitution was founded upon the Word of God, and it is absolutely essential that you do not allow anything or anyone to change that which was written. Open your mouth and call on the name of Jesus. If the people of America keep silent to that which is right, then you will lose everything. The wealth of this country will be transferred to another nation, but this is not the will of the Father. It is essential for you to keep that which was written and to not allow it to be altered or watered down.

A people who know their God shall have great

exploits. Nothing will ever be hidden or taken away. In my six years of living in a country that has such treasure, never have I experienced such a gem. I suppose those of you living in a country of wealth do not appreciate and value that which you have. I am here to tell you that it is time to pray. As I worshipped in praise a few days ago, I felt so impressed by the Holy Spirit to write down the following: "Tell the people of America far and near to pray for their commander in chief, pray for the armed forces, pray for the ground troops and their families, pray for the police force, and pray for the firefighters."

At first I asked, "Lord, the commander in chief?" Then as I repeated what He told me, it became apparent that this was the president. I felt an urgency to relay this message. As I started praying again, I heard how the people of America and all countries need to be alert. "Lord, what are you saying? I feel so helpless! I am a small fish in a very large sea. What do you want me to do?" After opening my eyes quickly and pausing for a moment, I thought, *God, the task you have given me is great, and I know you will guide me, so I will be obedient.* I closed my eyes and started praying.

Then I heard again, "The people of America need to rise up and pray for the country. Pray for states and cities, especially New York and Washington D.C. Pray for what is happening in other countries, and pray that the right decisions will be made. Pray that there will be no retaliation, and pray that a hedge of protection surrounds America. Pray Isaiah 54:17—'No weapon that is formed against thee shall prosper; and every tongue that shall rise against thee in judgment thou shalt condemn. This is the heritage of the servants of the Lord, and their righteousness is of me, saith the Lord.' Pray that the young people in colleges and universities will not be used by the evil one to create destruction and violence in the land. Pray that sleepers will not awake, and pray that if they arise, they will be confused and disarmed, and their works stopped, in the name of Jesus."

Isaiah 59:19 states, "So shall they fear the name of the Lord from the west and his glory from the rising of the Sun, when the enemy comes in like a flood, the Spirit of the Lord shall lift up a standard against him." I read that approximately 70–80 percent of Christians live in America. If this were true and everyone started praying—wow, what an effect. Nothing could penetrate the walls of protection. The angels would surround this beautiful country, and nothing could come in. If the people of God would unite in prayer regardless of denomination or title, recognize the importance of prayer right now, and begin to pray for America, just imagine the effect it would make. The crime rate would certainly decrease, and the movement of God would be evident. I feel there needs to be a regular vigil of prayer at the White House, where people are consistently interceding on behalf of those appointed into office, praying that God's will be done with everyone making important decisions that will affect the people of America. It takes love, consistency, and determination to say that we will not allow anything to happen to such a great nation. Whatever it takes, we are prepared to do it.

I saw in the Spirit the story of the Passover. Do you remember in the Bible, when the death angel went into Egypt, and the blood that was over the doorpost saved everyone in that house? Exodus 12:13 states, "And the blood shall be to you for a token upon the houses where ye are: and when I see the blood, I will pass over you, and the plague shall not be upon you to destroy you, when I smite the land of Egypt." This is what I see in the Spirit. People need to take time out to pray for their families and friends, to spend quality time loving and appreciating the families that God has given them, and to never take what they have for granted. Before going out in the mornings, plead the blood of Jesus (which is a prayer of protection) over your spouse and children. Pray against any disaster, violence, or crime. Pray Psalm 91. Be consistent and allow God to have His way. There is power in the blood of Jesus. Plead the blood of Jesus over your life, over your family and friends, and over your house. Come on, now. Get that anointed oil and place it over your front and back doors. Walk around your house and plead the blood of Jesus. Tell me, who can come against you when you are covered in the blood of Jesus? Wake up! Wake up! Jesus paid the price, and you have the authority in the name of Jesus. Pray!

There is an urgency and a reason why the Lord would have me write this book. It is so important to let you know that life is precious and that we have a God who is able to do the impossible. He is able to counteract the plans of every evil. He is able to stop and cancel every plan of the enemy. If people are obedient in praying and seeking the face of God, they will hear from heaven.

Notes

Revival!

I believe that a revival is about to break out! Suddenly, we will see the movement of God like never before.

> And it shall come to pass afterward, that I will pour out my spirit upon all flesh; and your sons and your daughters shall prophesy, your old men shall dream dreams, your young men shall see visions: And also upon the servants and upon the handmaids in those days will I pour out

my spirit. And I will shew wonders in the heavens and in the earth, blood, and fire, and pillars of smoke. (Joel 2:28–30)

Do not allow anything to stop you from praying and seeking the face of God. Do not fight evil with evil, but overcome it with prayer. Use prayer as a weapon to come against the enemy. Do not open yourself for attack. Speak peace, pray peace, and let God have His way. The Lord is America's shepherd, and we shall want of nothing—if the nation rises up in prayer. Look to God Almighty for the answer; He will always make a way. Lift up your eyes unto the hills like in Psalm 121.

Listen—can you hear the sound of the abundance of rain? Can you hear God calling you to pray? All-night prayer meetings are what we need. Open the closed church doors and let us pray. If you are a pastor, bishop, evangelist, or apostle, God is holding us accountable. Call the people of God together and pray. Spend quality time in the presence of the Lord. We need to hear from God *for such a time as this.* It is not about you. It is not about the material things of this life. It is not about money. When death draws near, can money save you? If death is about to knock at your door, and God is saying to pray, why would you ignore the voice of God? Call the intercessors; the prophets must arise. God is rising up the remnants: those who have been praying in the closets, those who have been groaning in the spirit, those who have been wailing and crying out to God. We are about to see the move of God. Position yourself in prayer. Turn off the television, switch off your cell phone, get into your closet, and get into the presence of God now!

Can you see what is happening? The enemy is

trying to create fear all over the world. More and more lives are being taken in our communities, cities, and countries. People are becoming more fearful, angry, and resentful. Some want to retaliate, but how can one fight evil with evil? The answer comes when a nation says, "Enough is enough. We do not have the answer so come let us pray." Pray Psalm 23. "Yea thou I walk through the valley of the shadow of death I will fear no evil for the Lord God Almighty is with me." Let God's will be done on earth as it is in heaven. Truly, is there anything that our God cannot do when we call on His name? "Behold, I am the LORD, the God of all flesh: is there anything too hard for me?" (Jer. 32:27).

I have found that the more time I spend in the presence of God, the more He speaks to me, giving me direction and instruction. I don't need to run to different places to hear a prophetic word. When God wants to confirm what He has said to me, He will send me to the right place at the right time. He will allow me to meet someone who is on point and on time with the word that comes forth, and for that I say, "Thank You, Jesus." He always brings confirmation. Any word that comes from God will not make you confused, angry, or stressed. How can you get a word from God and become confused? The devil is a liar. To truly hear from God, you must spend time praying. Then you will be able to discern that which is of God and that which is not of Him. You will know the difference between motivational speaking and God talking. When a prophet speaks from the throne room, you will know they are truly hearing from God. Pray for revival. Pray, repent, and confess. Pray the prayer of Daniel 9:3–19. "We have sinned, and have committed iniquity, and have done wickedly, and have rebelled, even by departing from thy precepts and from thy judgments."

Lord, I will run to you. Oh Lord, forgive, do not delay. Oh, that we will see the hand of God moving in our lives and in the lives of our community. Let us come against the territorial demons that are holding up our cities, our neighborhoods. Let's come against the spirit of death that is taking our young men and women. Have we become so immune to death that is has become acceptable and a way of life? Are you willing to stand in the gap and pray? When I hear the song "I Give Myself Away" by William McDowell, I am moved and say, "God, here I am. Use me." Allow God to use you. "The gates of hell shall not prevail."

It is time to see the Holy Ghost moving like you have never before in your life. When the Spirit of

God takes over our lives, our communities, and our countries, we will know that divine visitation took place. People will be crying out, falling on their faces, and calling on the name of Jesus. Those who never believed will say that they had a divine encounter with God.

Let the people who know God fast and pray. Deny yourself, take up your cross, and follow Jesus. There is something about the name Jesus; it is the sweetest name I know. In order for a revival, God is calling each of us to pray.

Notes

Fast and Pray

When the going gets tough, seek His face. I know it has been hard, and at times you thought you could not take it anymore. There seems to be lack in every area of your life. *Why?* You must have asked this question many times. *Why is this really happening?*

Someone once told me that he was tired of praying and felt that God had forgotten him. God is never late. He is an on-time God. Psalm 37:35 says, "I have been young and now am old, yet I have not seen the righteous forsaken or his seed begging bread."

Do you really think that God is going to leave you or forsake you? No way! It is not going to happen. God is with you. As you are reading this book, He is speaking, "It is well."

Let me pause for a moment and share a little of my story. My life was never an easy ride. At the age of nineteen, I was homeless. My mother believed it was time for me to leave home, even though I was not working; she literally threw my clothes out on the streets. I never intended to leave home then, but I decided that I would never return. I had done nothing wrong.

At the age of twenty-two, I suffered violently at the hands of my children's father. I was abused emotionally, verbally, and physically; I was raped; and I travelled the tunnel of death on more than one occasion. I ran for my life with my children and was homeless a second time, until finally purchasing my house and living for many years with my three children.

Being a single mother was not easy. I was hurt again and again by those whom I thought I could trust. I learned from a very young age to pray, and I always drew my strength in knowing that my God was my healer. He taught me not to be bitter but a better person. He also taught me what true love was all about, and He held me in the palm of His hands. When I thought, "God, I cannot take anymore," He touched me in the inward part, healing and restoring my broken heart and broken spirit.

I learned how to trust in Him, and I realized that I could not walk daily without the Lord holding my hand. In my midnight hours, I would draw strength from Jesus. When my back was against the wall, I would cry and cry until I thought I was all dried out, and my heavenly Father would be right there for me. I have been rejected by those near and far. I've been hated, abused, cursed, and told that I would never make it. But God, my one true friend, walked with me, talked with me, helped me, supported me, provided for me, and loved me. When I felt alone, He would always give me a word or a song in my lonely hours. When my children were going through what I would call their teenage crisis … but God. When I had no food … but God. When I was hurting … but God.

I have never done anything in my own strength. I have prayed and prayed, fasted and prayed, at times thirty days or longer. I have sought the face of God for my marriage, my children, my life, my family, my friends, my community, and my country. I have always found a "knee city" called prayer. There were many times when I could not share what was in my heart, and I spent days praying and praying, "I will not be denied what is mine!" Yes, my journey has been long, so I know what it is to pray. I know what it is to seek the face of God and see Him work in the most impossible situations. I have seen the hand of God in my life, and He has used me many times to speak the prophetic word. I have travelled and preached at conferences and churches of various denominations in different countries.

When God called me into ministry, it was after a long period of fasting and praying, seeking God. I had finished Bible college and was open to the leading of the Spirit. I heard the voice of God when He gave me the name of the ministry and told me what to do and how to do it. I had a blueprint of each department, from outreach to the children and the young people. I cried, started making excuses, and asked, "Lord, are You sure this is You?" I received confirmation after confirmation, and I could not resist the calling on my life. I had no money—nothing to start my ministry.

Then one day as I visited my niece, I walked out of her home. At the end of her road was a large building for lease, staring right at me. "That's your building!" God said. I got a bottle of anointed oil and began to claim the ground. I walked around the building, laying my hands by faith and calling on the name of Jesus. Within a short period of time, I was negotiating a lease offer. They reduced the amount requested and allowed me to acquire the property with no deposit and three months' free rent. Who could it be but Jesus? I had no down payment, yet God granted me favor. The property was delivered into my hands, and I moved in by faith. That is just one example of what happens when you fast and pray.

Another time, a minister was promoting a trip to the Holy Land, Jerusalem. Again, I had no money, but I desired to go. Although I was five months pregnant, I spoke it in the atmosphere that I would take this trip. Praise God—the entire trip was paid in full. I have testimonies after testimonies of what God has done. Lives have been saved and changed, burdens have been removed, and yokes have been destroyed. So I live prayer. I love to pray, even when words fail me. I pray, I praise, and I intercede.

This is the now time to pray. People all over the world need to experience the love of Jesus. When there is a change of heart, a total surrender, God will change every area of your life. Do you believe it? Do you believe that God can do the impossible? Is there anything too hard for our heavenly Father? Come on, now. Let us pray, declaring Psalm 51 over our life. Let us also repent for the sins of our fathers, according to the prayer of Daniel in chapter 9. Repent—yes, repent. Ask the Holy Spirit to revive you again. Bless the Lord.

Have you come to a place in your life when you know that there is much more to receive from God? You read the Word. You hear the Word preached. You believe the Word. You have faith in God. Then why is there a longing within to see more of the manifested glory of God? I believe it is time to see the hand of God moving in your life, like in the days of Moses, Daniel, Elijah, Paul, and Silas. God is calling people to pray and seek His face. Going to church for one or two hours per week is not enough! I call it a ritual, saying and doing the same thing but asking the Holy Spirit to lead. And if you do, when God really wants to show up, everyone in church begins looking at the time and thinking, "We have to leave now." Quench the Spirit? Sorry, God—we have no time to listen to what you have to say. Ouch!

In modern-day culture, the church has become a quick fix; everything must be instant. Tell the people what they want to hear. It is not about having a personal relationship with God. People are seeking to hear the prophetic word while their lifestyles are not one of holiness. They are expecting to see a mighty move of God and a divine impartation in their lives, but they have no substance, no relationship with Him. Everything is material based. A very well-known Pentecostal pastor, whom I loved very much growing up, once told a story of a rat that fell into some porridge. When the cook found it, he licked it dry and said, "Dry you fell in, and dry you shall return." The pastor used the rat to illustrate members' behavior in the church. "Dry you come, and dry you return."

When I heard that story as a young person, I thought it was quite hilarious. Now I understand perfectly what he meant. People go into the house of the Lord with a need: dry, hungry, wanting to see the move of God in their lives. Yet, they leave the house of God exactly the same—no change, no healing, no deliverance, no conviction, nothing after hearing the Word. It makes one wonder what is happening in the churches today. Are we not serving the same God of yesterday? Yes, we are. What do people need to do? Get back to basics and spend quality time in the presence of God.

I remember as a young person, the presence of God was always evident in the church. People were always on fire for God. Sometimes the fear of God would get hold of my heart, and I would be fearful to go into God's house because I knew I was not living right. I wonder if people are feeling that way today? Before they leave for church, are they thinking, "I need to repent and get right with God"?

There must a fear, a reverence, for holiness, as well as a desire to be in right standing with God.

Notes

Distractions

Have you ever found that when you try to pray, everything comes to distract you? Sometimes when I started praying, I would fall asleep on my knees, and I would wake up and start again. The devil is a liar. I would get into a fighting spirit and say, "This is it. I am not tired. I had a good night's rest. No way, Satan. You are not going to put the spirit of slumber and sleep upon me." I would start rebuking and I get back to praying. Now I turn off my cell phone and get rid of all distractions when I am going to talk to my Father.

What do you think hinders you from praying? I can start with laziness. People have become lazy and comfortable with their way of life; only when things get bad do they call on the name of Jesus. Watching the television has become the number one priority. How many times have you heard the Word and the Lord speak into your heart to pray? Time and time again, do you get distracted with the cares of this life? Minutes, hours, days, and months go by! Somehow things don't seem to get any better.

I want you to remember this: every time the evil spirit distracts you, you are missing out on your blessing. You are missing out on hearing a word from God. Every time you give way to the enemy, you are losing precious time walking and running into your divine destiny. Satan's job is to keep you from praying, to keep you from listening to and hearing from God. He wants to stop the gifts working within you, in order to create havoc in your life. There is power in praying, and he is trying to take the power. If you don't pray, you become weak. Make time! You have not made time to say, "Good morning, Holy Spirit."

Imagine that you wake up in the morning and begin your day without spending ten minutes or more praying and giving God thanks. I have found that the best time to pray is early morning, giving God the best part of your day. I set my alarm for 5:00 a.m., rise up, and pray. Everything for that day goes smoothly. I went to bed early, knowing that I had to spend time with my Father—quality time in God's presence. Have you found that at 3:00 a.m. and 5:00 a.m., you wake up for no apparent reason and struggle to go back to sleep? God is calling you to pray. Something is happening in the atmosphere, and you need to be praying. Do you know that at those times, the enemy is very active? That is why God is waking you up to pray.

Praying in the Spirit brings great result. Spend at least ten minutes praying in the spirit. Oh, my Lord. It is beautiful, and doors will begin to open. God is waiting for you to come. The songwriter Charlotte Elliott, puts it so eloquently: "Just as I am, without one plea and as the blood was shed for me and as thou bid me come. To thee, oh lamb of God I come, I come."

I have had many of those days when I could hear the call of God, knowing that I had to stop everything and spend time in prayer. This is not the time to get distracted or get off course. You cannot afford to waste time doing things that do not profit your soul. What will it profit to get distracted? The spirit of distraction. Lets' name a few.

- You are too tired to pray.
- Your cell phone interrupts you.
- An emergency arises that you must deal with immediately.
- Someone is in need of help.
- While praying, your thoughts are on the many things you have to do.

Sound familiar? The list goes on and on. Distractions will prevent you from receiving your blessing.

"Thou shalt have no other gods before me. Thou shalt not make unto thee any graven image, or any likeness of anything that is in heaven above, or that is in the earth beneath, or that is in the water under the earth. Thou shalt not bow down thyself to them, nor serve them: for I the LORD thy God am a jealous God." (Exod. 20:3–5, KJV)

Restoration

God is about to restore everything! You may have lost so much over the years: your marriage, money, home, job, friends, and loved ones. Oh, how it hurts—but you must believe that restoration is yours, in the name of Jesus. You must believe the years that the enemy has robbed from your life are about to come back to you. You are about to smile and laugh again.

It has been so long that you may find this hard to believe. Do you believe in the God of the impossible, the true and living God who is able to make the impossible possible? Believe, and you shall receive! Do you believe that God can and will do it? Stretch your faith and hold on, for you are going to smile and praise the name of Jesus. He is worthy of all the praise. Greatness is about to come forth from your life, so it is important that you spend time in prayer, positioning and preparing for what you are about to receive. Wealth transfer is coming your way, in the name of Jesus. What has been held up is about to be released to you, in Jesus's name. You will have so much financially that you will not know what to do. Start planning wisely for the overflow coming into your account. You do not want to miss out on what our heavenly Father has for you.

For years the people of God have been in bondage and have dealt with problem after problem. Hold on to the promises of God. After all, 2 Peter 3:9 says, "The Lord is not slack concerning His promise, as some men count slackness; but is longsuffering to us-ward, not willing that any should perish, but that all should come to repentance." Maybe you have felt that you have been robbed of your blessings; something always seems to happen when you're on the brink of your breakthrough. Everything falls apart into a disaster.

This would happen to me, and the Lord revealed to me the cause: witchcraft to hinder and stop me from receiving my blessings from God. I changed the way in which I prayed. I went into warfare praying. You have to change the way you pray. When you find that you are continually coming against walls of darkness, hindrances, and blockages, you have to use the weapon that has been given to you. Pray in a different way.

Decree that every destiny-altering spirit is cancelled over your life, in the name of Jesus. Declare that every negative word, spoken against your life is now impotent. Remove the sentence of death from your life and your loved ones, in the name of Jesus. Command the best to manifest, in the name of Jesus. Pray and cancel all demonic agendas and assignments of the enemy that have been sent by witches and warlocks to be destroyed from the root, in the name of Jesus. Send the fire of God on every evil spirit that comes to steal, kill, and destroy your life and your family's lives.

Don't play with the enemy. Remember, you have the power. Open your mouth and decree and declare in the name of Jesus. Pray divine manifestation like never before. Pray the Word of God over your life.

Plead the blood of Jesus. Apply the blood of Jesus over everything that you are about to do. Plead the blood daily over your family, your children, and your possessions in Jesus's name. Decree and declare manifestation and demonstration of the Holy Spirit. Ask God to stir up the gifts within you. Serve the enemy notice to get out of your life, your family's lives, your family, your community, and your church, in the name of Jesus. Take your inheritance by force. Glory be to God!

Do not keep your mouth shut and accept less. You will have the best and nothing less. This is your season, and it's a new day. There is an open heaven over your life. God is with you; believe and use the key of authority. "Whatever you bind on earth is bound in heaven and whatever you loose on earth is loosed in heaven" (Matt. 18:18). The power of darkness cannot stand when you pray. A nation will rise up when you pray. Revival will come forth when you pray. The enemy cannot and will not stop you from finishing your race when you pray. There will be no premature deaths in the name of Jesus. Nothing can hold you captive when you pray. Every frustration of the past is broken now to be lifted in the name of Jesus.

Do not be sad of what you have lost; think on what you are about to gain. Begin to praise the name of Jesus. Praise Him in the morning, and praise Him all day. Make a joyful noise unto the Lord. God will show himself strong and mighty in your life. Decree and declare heaven's best to come to you, and it shall happen in the name of Jesus. God is about to restore the years that were stolen from you (Joel 2:25). God will give back to you more than you ever had in your life. Pray and repent, asking God to forgive you for being too busy. Pray Psalm 51. There needs to be a humble submission before God, acknowledging that you have fallen short, messed up, and gone your own way far too long. It is time for you to forget the things of the past. The bondage of all the past hurt and pain is holding you captive and robbing you of your blessing. Let go and let God have His way in your life.

I was so broken, rejected by someone I loved very much. I could not forgive him for a very long time. I kept saying over and over, "I did not deserve to be treated badly." I felt I was a good person. How could anyone be so unjust to me?

Then one day the Lord said, "How long are you going to hold this person ransom? You have locked them up and thrown away the key. Why? When are you going to move on? You have caged them up in your heart and have refused to let them go. You must let go now!"

For days I cried and prayed, asking God to forgive me and help me to forgive. Soon I felt such a release in my life, and the love that I had in my heart was unexplainable. You may be asking, "How can you begin to forget the past?" I have learned to allow the Holy Spirit to fill me with His love and peace. "What a friend we have in Jesus all our sins and grief to bear what a privilege it is to carry everything to Him in prayer." Allow the Lord to heal and restore the years that the enemy has stolen. "So I will restore to you the years that the swarming locust has eaten the crawling locust: the consuming locust, and the chewing locust" (Joel 2:25).

Many years ago, so much was stolen from me. I was in the process of moving, but I had nowhere to store my possessions until the house was ready. A sister in the church said I could store everything in her garage. I was so grateful that she had such a lovely heart to help. Within four months, I obtained my house and drove to her place, excited to get all by belongings. However, she walked me to the garage, and to my horror everything was gone except a few boxes of books. It was beyond belief. I could only smile as she told me some story about rain destroying my things … but it was amazing that the books had not been damaged. As I walked away, my driver asked, "Are you going to say or do anything?"

I said, "No. God will restore all that the enemy has stolen." And guess what? The Lord restored everything that I had lost—and more.

Are you trying every method possible to be free? The only way freedom will truly come into your life is by spending time in prayer. God is waiting for you to come to Him. His Word will come forth, and you will know for sure that the Spirit of the Lord God is upon your life. God, Yahweh, our Father and Friend is about to do a supernatural work in your life. Do not give up when you're on the brink of your miracle. God is calling you to a higher place in Him. "For you shall know the truth and the truth shall make you free (John 8:32)."

Do not divorce if you know in your heart your marriage is God ordained. This is a tactic that the enemy is using to break the family unit. Why not prove God? Do you know love will conquer the force of evil? Spend time loving on Jesus, and let the love of God flow from you to your spouse. Let the love of God prevail, even when you feel the person does not deserve it. Let go and let God speak into your heart.

Let Him touch you and give you peace. Only God can heal the broken-hearted. It may seem impossible, but God is about to turn it around, healing and restoring your marriage. Your husband is coming back; your wife is coming home. Your children will be saved in the name of Jesus.

You may think that there is no hope for your children and that they are beyond changing. You may be a single parent struggling with your children. They may seem to be out of control, and you may be thinking, "I don't know what to do." Your answer today is prayer. Pray for your son or your daughter. If the enemy can destroy the seed that will bruise the serpent's head, then he has won the battle. No way! You cannot wrestle in the flesh. This is what the evil one wants you to do. Get a piece of clothing—anything that belongs to your son or daughter, husband or wife—and use it as a point of contact. Every day, decree and declare using the word. Command and demand in the name of Jesus. I guarantee you that change will come into your house. Do not pray over them for a few days and stop; consistency is the key to success. You must keep it up, even when you do not have the energy to say another word. Keep going.

As I started to do this, things would seem to get worse to make me feel like giving up. Instead, I would get on my knees and pray even more. Many years ago, my son was on the streets with friends that I did not approve of, so I decided enough was enough. Every time he went out, I was on my knees, praying. I would get his T-shirt, and I would cry and pray. I would walk the streets, praying and splashing the ground with anointed oil. One day, he saw me in the distance and hid inside a store. When I got close, I asked his friends where he was, and they lied. I was not silent, and I pleaded the blood over them, commanding the devil to take his hand off my son. Looking back, my son must have thought, "My mum is crazy!"

I used to say this all the time, "I will not be denied what is mine." You will not be denied of what is yours! The devil is a liar. Get your boxing gloves on and begin to fight. You are in spiritual warfare. Fight! If you find it difficult to pray alone, or it is overwhelming, start a prayer meeting in your home or at church. Get others to come in agreement with you in prayer at least once a week. Start a prayer line, getting friends and family members to join you in prayer. It makes a difference.

About a year ago, the Lord laid on my heart to start a prayer line. I did not know how I was going to begin, but God said to create a Skype prayer line. I started by faith, and today we have many people from several different countries, and we have had some very powerful testimonies. It is time to be obedient and pray. Your family and friends will be delivered from every addiction, in the name of Jesus. The gang member will accept the Lord Jesus Christ. Jesus said it! Believe it and receive it in the name of Jesus. Depression and oppression will be gone in the name of Jesus! "When the spirit of the Lord comes upon my heart, I will dance like David danced." You will be singing and dancing and praising the name of the Lord.

Families are about to be healed and restored, delivered and set free. Your sons and daughters will be saved. It shall come. The Bible says, "That if you shall confess with thy mouth the Lord Jesus, and shall believe in your heart, that God hath raised Him from the dead, you shall be saved" (Rom. 10:9).

If you have been praying for a breakthrough, it is up to you to make time and spend time in the presence of God. There is a work that He has for you to do, and the time is now. I never knew I could write poetry. I never imagined that I would be able to write books, have business ideas, and be creative. God knew. Everything about me came forth in prayer. I studied and passed many exams, even though I thought I could not do it. Every time I prayed, the Lord told me what I had to do. I would take a step of faith and say, "God, You said … I believe You have already made the way." I walked by faith, and every time God helped me. Nothing is impossible with God.

The only way that you will get your breakthrough is by praying and spending time in the word of God. Then He will tell you what to do in order to receive deliverance. Please know it is not always the way you think is going to happen. Read the Word, live by the Word, and let the Lord guide you every minute of the day. When you allow the Holy Spirit to guide you, how can you go wrong? The Bible says, "The steps of a good man are ordered by the LORD: and he delights in his way" (Ps. 37:23). Again, there is nothing impossible with God, if only you believe. "And Jesus said unto them, Because of your unbelief: for verily I say unto you, If ye have faith as a grain of mustard seed, ye shall say unto this mountain, Remove hence to yonder place; and it shall remove; and nothing shall be impossible unto you"(Matt. 17:20). "When you call He will answer and show you great and mighty things, which you know not" (Jer. 33:3).

Salvation is amazing, wonderful, awesome, unending love. God's love is very real, and nothing can compare to the love of God.

"For God so loved the world that He gave His only begotten Son that whosoever believeth in Him should not perish but have everlasting life." (John 3:16)

At the age of eighteen, I gave my heart to the Lord, and I knew that God's hand was upon my life. I was a very rebellious teenager. I loved fighting, especially if others got in my way. Trouble would always seem to find me; I didn't need to look for it. I can only but smile at this point. I was never afraid to stand my ground. I was suspended from my school on more than one occasion. I remember the first day my mother took me to school. When I was about to go on the playground, she said, "If anyone bothers you at school, take off your shoes and beat them." With this statement in my mind, a child came up to me on the playground, and sure enough, she started to bother me. What did I do? Yes, you guessed right. The consequence for my action on my very first day was getting the cane on my hand. That is when it all started.

My bad attitude and bad behavior went with me into high school. My parents were at a stage of not knowing what would become of me. The church that my parents attended came together and prayed. They organized to send me to a Christian summer camp. Thinking I was going to have fun, I agreed to go, oblivious to the fact that they had spent time fasting and praying for me. The stage was set; all I had to do was attend. Sure enough, God answered their prayer. This young teenage girl, who was adamant that she was going to leave camp no different, gave her heart to the Lord. Prayer works.

I still remember when the Word was preached on the fifth day, a Thursday evening, around a campfire. I was lifting my hand in the air, without any hesitation,

I wanted Jesus in my life. Prayer will make the impossible possible. God will always answer, and He is always on time. Do not expect things to happen in your time. Remember this: God is never late. Maybe that would explain why I have such a love in my heart for children and young people: I simply enjoy having them around me. God has given me a compassionate spirit. It does not bother me if they are challenging, bad, or indifferent because I know that if I pray, God can deliver. Someone can say, "No way. I will never give my heart to the Lord." Just keep praying. The person will be saying yes tomorrow. God can touch people at their point of need.

When a church of sincere Christians had enough of a rebellious, uncontrollable teenager and wanted to see change, what did they do? They prayed! When you listen to the news today, more and more young people are dying. It is going to take the people of God to come together and say, "Enough is enough. We are tired of what is happening in our families, in our communities, in our cities, and in our countries."

The young people shall not die, but they shall live and declare the works of the Lord. They will become evangelists, teachers, pastors, prophets, and apostles. Doctors, pilots, presidents, engineers, and more shall rise up in the name of Jesus.

Let us pray and seek the face of God on behalf of our youth. Let us unite and intercede, until we see a change. Revival must come forth. God does answer prayers; He will take people out of the clubs and off the streets. He'll even wake them up out of their sleep. If they are high on drugs, God will heal. They will know the power of God is real! The gunmen, drug dealers, and gang leaders will run into the presence of God. Our Father, who art in heaven, the almighty King of kings and Lord of lords, is about to show up in the lives of thousands of our young people all over the world. The chain of darkness will be broken, and there will be a move of God like we have never seen in our lifetime.

God will do a new thing when the people of God cry out to Him to save our young people. Go into the enemies' camp and pray them out of hell, in the name of Jesus. Someone has to make that sacrifice. Someone has to call the people together and say, "Come, let us pray." My journey has been a life of prayer. Have I always gotten it right? Not always, but God has never failed in speaking to me. At times when I thought He was nowhere to be found, He reassured me that He is always there. All I have to do is reach out for the Word, and every time God has spoken. Prayer has taken me to places that I never dreamt possible. Never in a million years did I dream of living in America. God ordained it before the foundation of the earth.

In 1988, I travelled to the Holy Land, Jerusalem. Doors were open for me to visit this beautiful country, to walk the path that our Lord and Savior, Jesus Christ, walked. I ministered in India for fifteen days, and this experience would not have happened without prayer. I spent time with people who have a hunger and thirst for God. When you begin to seek the Lord with all of your heart, be consistent and do not give up. Do not go off-track—run the race and keep the pace. The Holy Spirit will begin to tell you what to do. There will be such a peace in your heart that you know you are doing the right thing.

The spirit of the Lord God is upon you, because the Lord has anointed you to preach good tidings to the poor; He has sent you to heal the brokenhearted to proclaim liberty to the captives, and the opening of the prison to those who are bound: to proclaim the acceptable year of the Lord and the day of vengeance of our God. To comfort all who mourn in Zion: To give them beauty for ashes. The oil of joy for mourning. The garment of praise for the spirit of heaviness; that they may be called trees of righteousness, the planting of the Lord, that he may be glorified. (Isa. 61:1–3)

Notes

Be Obedient!

About fourteen years ago, while praying, the Lord told me that He wanted me to go into the inner city, on a particular street that is known as the front line in England, at midnight a week before the New Year. God revealed to me that something bad was about to happen in the New Year, and I had to anoint and pray for the men, especially the Jamaican men. I knew that on a Friday night, there would be a lot of activity on what is called the front line, or red light area (i.e., prostitution, drug dealing, and late-night parties). The Lord was very precise in His instructions. I should take someone with me, as well as a bottle of anointed oil, and anoint all the men, especially the Jamaican men.

Doubt immediately crept in. "God, is this you?" Instantly I felt the peace of God. I knew that God was with me. I asked one of my church sisters to come with me, and she agreed. We started walking from the top of the street, and with all the people we met, I asked politely if I could anoint them and pray. They were open and willing to be prayed for, and I was a little surprised. But why should I have been surprised? God had already opened the way for us. Only one person said no.

We prayed until finally we stood outside a building that is known by everyone in the city. It's not the best place to be seen inside or outside, especially after midnight. We stood outside and prayed, and as the men came out, we prayed until the Lord said it was done.

The first week of January, war broke out between individuals and two gangs. The police and the army had to be called out, patrolling the very street to which the Lord had sent me. Needless to say, the end result was not good. What was known as the front line was now taken over by the police. Throughout the city, it was a danger zone. This was the main headline news for local newspapers and radio stations for many weeks after New Year's.

Today, that road is no longer known as front line, and the building we visited was demolished. However, many of the men whom I had prayed for were nowhere to be found. They had escaped all the destruction that had taken place.

It is important to walk in obedience. When God tells you to do something, although you may not understand, simply walk in obedience. God has already made a way, and you could be saving a life. God will take you out of your comfort zone and allow you to do tasks that you never thought you would be able to do. He will give you confidence and boldness to go and do His will. As you get out of your comfort zone, you will be amazed how He uses you.

The Lord told me a few months ago that there is absolutely nothing that He cannot do. He is my helper. All I need to do is ask, and He will do it. I remember one day I needed a jacket, but shopping is not one of my hobbies; I am usually in and out within an hour. However, on this particular day, I simply could not find one that I needed for the next day. Finally, after no success I felt very frustrated. I stood for a moment and asked the Holy Spirit to lead me to a jacket. Within seconds of asking, I found myself walking to a rail and reaching for a jacket. Amen, it was on sale! I could only smile and say, "Thank You, Lord. You are awesome. You are wonderful."

On another occasion, I was about to travel abroad to minister when the Lord woke me up and said, "Today, you are going to buy yourself some suits."

I thought, "Suits, Lord? I do not have enough money to buy suits." Then He told me exactly where to go. "All right, Lord." Sure, enough, I found two suits, and both were on sale. I started laughing. There is nothing God cannot handle. "If ye shall ask any thing in my name, I will do it" (John 14:14). Sometimes when you pray, doubt creeps in. That's when it is essential to know and use the Word. Begin to decree and declare all that you believe God does on your behalf.

Many years ago, I was in church praying for many hours, and I clearly heard the Lord tell me to go to a local restaurant and speak to the business owner, because he was about to give up the shop. I immediately telephoned my sister, the main chef of the family, and told her what the Lord had said about taking over the restaurant. I went by faith and met the owner's brother, who confirmed that his brother was indeed about to give it up. I made arrangements to meet with the owner, and the rest is history. It is owned by a member of my family to this very day. You cannot fail with prayer.

The Lord brought to my remembrance a film The Dark Knight. I had watched with Batman, Joker, and a very good attorney whose life changed when the one he loved was killed. His world fell apart, but more important, the Joker had pushed him so far that he was now killing others. He did not care anymore about his actions or about anything that he had accomplished in the past. He was so angry, hurt, and bitter. The Joker almost won what he had set out to do, which was to conquer good, until the attorney who had fallen from grace was made a hero instead.

As I thought about the movie, I recognize that is exactly what the enemy wants the people of God to do: doubt, give up, stop believing that God is able, and waste time feeling sorry for themselves. The people of God need to walk by faith, pray, and not be moved by disappointment. Keep pressing, regardless of what happens in life. Good has to come forth. Do not be moved by what you see or how you feel, but by the Spirit of God. You will testify of the goodness of Jesus. You will overcome not by might nor by power, but by His Spirit (Zech. 4:6).

You may be feeling that all is lost. Well, you are reading this book for a reason. There is hope, and better and best are coming your way. You cannot and will not be moved by how you are feeling right now. Do not allow your emotions to dictate your actions and the decisions you make. Allow Jesus, to guide you and help you every minute of the day. Sure enough, He will always make a way when there seems to be no way.

Witchcraft

Witchcraft is real. Oh, that the people of God would wake up to what is happening around them and see the forces that are fighting against them every day. Remember, "We do not wrestle against flesh and blood but against principalities, against powers, against the rulers of the darkness of this age, against spiritual hosts of wickedness in the heavenly places" (Eph. 6:12). We must put on the whole armor of God to stand against the wiles of the devil. The war is not to be fought in the flesh but in the Spirit. Recognize that every day, you are fighting a demon that comes in all shapes and sizes. You must be able to discern when you are fighting against principalities, against powers, and against the rulers of the darkness of this age. Know who you are in Christ Jesus.

One day I began asking the question, "Why is it that every time I put one foot forward to do the will of God, everything seems to go wrong?" Witchcraft! Do you know that the enemy creates a diversion for you to be distracted? He hates when you are focused and praying consistently. Witchcraft is real, assignments are real, and attacks are real. The devil sends out his imps, demons, and spiritual attacks, by using a close friend, family member, or someone we love. People may start verbally attacking you for no reason, or they may accuse, abuse, or draw you into something that is really not your problem but becomes your problem, which then has a major impact on your emotions. Then they add the feelings of anger, bitterness, resentment, destruction, stress, or death. Oh, yes, do not forget that depression does not want to be left out of the mix. All are the influence of witchcraft.

This is when the spirit of God must arise in you and allow the evil one to scatter, in the name of Jesus. "Let God arise." You will not be denied. Come on, now. "If God be for you who can be against you?" (Ro. 8:31). One day, my husband had gone to work, and I started my daily chores in the house. Suddenly, I felt the force of darkness come into my home like never before. I could not breathe. I felt my body getting weak, and I could not do anything to stop the uncontrollable feeling. The more tried to get a grip with what was happening, the more I felt as though life was leaving my body. My spirit was very much alive, but my body felt weak. At one point, my heart was beating so fast that I thought I was having a heart attack, but I had no pain. I felt a sudden panic, but I had nothing about which to panic.

The more I questioned the attack, the more I could not walk, so I picked up my cell phone and texted the people of God to pray now. I stood with my back against the wall in my kitchen with tears in my eyes. By this time, I had telephoned my husband at work and asked him to come home. Then I heard the voice of God, the Spirit of the Lord, say, "Repeat Psalm 27, and do not stop." I began to recite all fourteen verses over and over, until I felt a shift in the atmosphere, a shift in my body. I was able to telephone my sister in England and explain what had taken place. Immediately she started to pray, and the Lord said to me, "Take Holy Communion." With my sister on the telephone, we did this together.

After we finished, I felt the power of God move in my dining room. I saw the angels of God, my warring angels, descending and fighting the forces of darkness. There was a shift! The forces of darkness, witchcraft, satanic assignments, and attacks were destroyed. I felt a release in my body. There was total freedom; I had victory. Praise the name of Jesus!

On another occasion, my husband had once again gone to work. As I entered my utility room I was confronted with flies. The door was white, but looked black because it was covered with blue bottle flies. There was no movement, I was shocked. Imagine a horror movie opening of a door and suddenly confronted with large flies. This time I knew that I had to allow God to rise up within and allow God to fight on my behalf. I called upon the warring angels, and they came to my rescue. I soaked my house with so much anointed oil that I saw flies dropping to the floor. Yes, they were under my feet when my husband arrived home from work. He was so shocked because he had never seen anything like it. There was nothing in that area to attract flies, but after using the oil and praying the Word (no fly spray), they were gone in the name of Jesus. I prayed Psalm 27, Psalm 23, and Psalm 35. I was later told by a pastor that it was an assignment from hell.

There is power in the name of Jesus to break every assignment of witchcraft. Both incidents were assignments sent to destroy my marriage. If you are married and experiencing problems after problems in your marriage, be aware that the enemy is after marriages. However, I decided to fight for my marriage on my knees. I made up my mind that I was not going to be denied of what was mine. When everything came for me to throw in the towel, the Lord said to me, "Do not take the actions of the world. Be still and do My will." That was my greatest test—being still and not saying a word. It was hard. I was hurting and crying, or I should say bawling. God said, "Be still." I would close my door and spend hours, day and night, on my knees, crying out to God.

Praise God, my change came. Yes, it happened, and I was truly praising the name of Jesus. I put on my fighting spirit. I was not about to give up anything that was mine. No way! I was going to see the hand of God in my life. Yes, I have come a very long way, and I suppose that is why the Lord would have me write about it today. I have sure been through the valley of the shadow of death, and for a split second, fear rose up in me.

Then God said, "Sound the battle cry! Put on your armor so that you will be able to stand. You will win this one. The battle is not yours—it is Mine. Love even when you don't feel like loving. Do not hate; do not be bitter. Love and love and love. Allow Me to take control of your mind, soul, and body. Allow Me to touch you where it hurts. Allow Me to be your husband and friend. Allow Me to comfort you and hold you in the palm of My hand. No man will snatch you out of My hand. Trust that I will take care of you. I will never leave you or forsake you." After hearing the voice of God, I dried my tears.

I am here to tell you that if you are going through a painful time in your life, do not dwell on it. Do not allow it to overtake you. You must love. If people hurt you, love them. Yes, love them. Turn it over to Jesus, and everything will be all right. When the forces of darkness come against you, use the Word to take authority over the situation. Witchcraft will always want to isolate you. Isolation is a sign that witchcraft is active around you. The devil, the evil one, will take over your mind if you allow him. You may find yourself having a pity party: "Poor me. No one cares. I am not loved; I am always hurting. Everything always happen to me. I am not beautiful or handsome. My life is so boring. I will never make it. I am a failure, and life is not worth living. I have always been rejected."

This is your imagination. The evil one will try to convince you that it is true—that your life is in turmoil. The main controlling demons are at work. Low self-esteem and fear creep in, and before long, every dirty little imp is having a party in your mind because you have opened the doorway.

This is where you must take hold of the Word of God and say, "The Lord is my shepherd I shall not want.... Greater is He that is in me than he that is in the world ... No weapon that is formed against me shall prosper, in the name of Jesus. I have been redeemed by the blood of the lamb, Jesus Christ."

The devil is a liar. Do not accept his lies, in the name of Jesus. Use the Word over and over again. Decree and declare; give no place to the enemy. Cover your mind in the blood of Jesus Christ.

"The WORD is a lamp to my feet, and
a light to my path." (Ps. 119:105)

Territorial Demons

I have learned a great deal and have come to realize that "Knee City" is the best place to be. Do not take your eyes off Jesus. Wherever you live, there are various levels of territorial demons that you have to face. For a prolonged period of time, I was dreaming death (which was active in the area I was living). After waking up, I would always encounter bad news, be it financial or otherwise. It was time to wage war, so I began to pray in my house, declaring the Word. Before I went to bed, I asked the Lord to send His warring angels to fight on my behalf. I made an appointment with God every morning at five to pray for an hour. For nearly two months, I would take Holy Communion every day. Yes, there was a change! I also began to sow into ministries, believing God for my breakthrough. Sure enough, everything for which I believed God came to pass.

You must be prepared to make the sacrifice in order to reap the reward. There is no quick fix in spiritual warfare. You must be prepared to fight, and determined that you will not be denied of what is yours. You will have heaven's best and nothing less. God has ordained it, and it will come to pass. Far too many have gone to be with the Lord, and they never fulfilled all that they were called to do. You were born to praise the name of Jesus. You were born to pray and to have fellowship with God. You were born to walk into your purpose and live to your full potential. Why, then, would you allow the evil one to rob you of what is yours?

Do not allow the envy and evil of others to prevent you. Do not allow the darts and arrows of the evil one to stop you. Do not allow the words of man to slow you down. I rebuke every curse back to the pit of hell, in the name of Jesus. God has blessed you, and who God has blessed, no man can curse. Rebuke the plans of the devil, in the name of Jesus. God is with you. If you believe, you will pursue, overtake, and recover all in the name of Jesus. Your future is bright and getting brighter every minute. Praise the name of Jesus. Because He lives, you can face tomorrow, and the next day. Laugh at the enemy. Come on, now—laugh. You are about to possess all in the name of Jesus.

Revival is coming forth in the name of Jesus. Revival, revival! At the name of Jesus, every knee shall bow; it shall come to pass. There will be an outpouring of the Spirit of God on those who have called on the name of Jesus. You will see with your eyes and hear with your ears the reward of the wicked, in the name of Jesus. Increase shall come forth! Signs and wonders shall follow the people of God—those who have presented themselves as a living sacrifice unto the Lord. Oh, praise the name of Jesus!

A Life of Faith

You must have faith in the impossible. Believe by faith that God is going to do it, regardless of what is happening. The reason I am stressing this point is because so many are throwing in the towel. I have heard of many believers giving into temptation, and others are not bothering to pray or read the Word because they have become tired of being tired. The Lord told me I should not confess to the enemy that I was tired. I should refrain from saying, "I am tired."

People have been going through problems day after day and not getting any closer to a release. Many have become busy doing other things. The cares of this life have taken first place, and there is no longer a hunger and thirst for righteousness. They no longer seek the face of God because their focus is on paying the bills, going to work, making money, and possessing material things. Their love for God has gone cold. They are not prepared in the spirit, and so they cannot see when the enemy is firing his darts every day. The blind is leading the blind into hell.

More and more people, especially our young people, are accepting darkness rather than light. Witchcraft seems to be acceptable because it is shown more and more in the media (e.g., films, cartoons, and children's programs). There seem to be more *good* witches! This is a lie from the pit of hell, making it seem acceptable for adults and children alike. No one questions and stops their children from watching these cartoons, because it is a way to keeping them quiet. People of God, wake up and realize that we are in the end-time. It is written. "If my people, which are called by my name, shall humble themselves, and pray, and seek my face, and turn from their wicked ways; then will I hear from heaven, and will forgive their sin, and will heal their land" (2 Chron. 7:14).

A few nights ago, I had a dream, and the Lord told me that it was important for His people to spend time in prayer, because only when I pray is He able to lift up a standard against the enemy. Only then is He able to send His angels of protection and His warring angels to help His people and deliver them from all evil. "So shall they fear the name of the LORD from the west, and his glory from the rising of the sun.

When the enemy shall come in like a flood, the Spirit of the LORD shall lift up a standard against him" (Isa. 59:19). It is not over until God says it is over.

I hear in the Spirit that people of God are becoming weary and tired of fighting. They have lost their joy and strength. Remember this: "Do not grieve, for the joy of the LORD is your strength" (Neh. **8:10**). Jesus will deliver you. Nothing is impossible. You will speak to that mountain, and it will be removed. It is time! Believe that you have the authority that Jesus has given to you to come against that which is hindering you.

The Lord told me quite recently that I was going to England. I did not know how it was going to happen, but I started to pack my suitcase by faith, believing God for the finances. Although I did not have much, I sowed into a TV ministry by faith. I knew it was

God leading me to sow, and before long, I received the finances in my account. I went online and found a flight, but when I entered all my bank details and clicked submit, nothing happened. I began praying and pleading the blood, in the name of Jesus. Then the words "Internet connection unplugged" popped up on my computer screen. I said, "The devil is a liar." I checked and double-checked all connections, and everything was perfectly fine. I started the process all over again. Praise the Lord, I booked my flight for the next day. I was delighted and ready to go.

That evening, I thought, *Let me take my passport and put it safely in my hand luggage.* Oh, no! No passport! This was not possible. I have never in my life misplaced my passport. I had just traveled a few weeks prior. Two hours passed, and I still could not find it. By this time, all my paperwork, books, and files were on the floor. My room looked as if there had been an earthquake. Tears started flowing because I could not understand where my passport could be. After having searched everywhere possible, I got rid of unwanted paperwork in the process and put everything back in its proper place. "God, where is it?" More than three hours passed, and it was getting late. I needed to get some rest to travel early the next day.

Then the Spirit of God rose up inside of me, and I said, "This is it! Before midnight, I need to find my passport." I went on my knees and prayed, "Lord, I give up. I leave everything in Your hands. Let Your will be done. If You do not want me to go to England, that is fine. But if You want me to go, please show me where my passport is now!" I got up from my knees, walked into my living room, and sat down on my sofa. Within a few minutes of sitting quietly,

I heard the voice of God telling me exactly where to look. I walked back into the bedroom as instructed, and there was my passport, staring right at me in the place where my Father told me to look! I was amazed because I had already spent so much time looking in this very spot and had carefully put everything back. Now, there it was looking right at me. How could this be? I smiled and thanked God for hearing my prayer and answering so quickly.

Faith! You must believe when God speaks to you. Believe and walk by faith, knowing that God already has the answer for you.

Several years ago, my husband and I were living in a very uncomfortable environment. One day I woke up and declared in the atmosphere, "I will be moving by the end of the month. I will not live like this any longer. Enough is enough! I am a child of God, and I will not settle for less than the best." Within a week, my husband came home with good news of additional finances from work, which meant we could move. Not knowing the areas very well, I went on the Internet and began searching for a new home. I found two houses and decided to go for the one that was a lot closer to my husband's employment, but the Lord said no. He told me to go for the other house and granted me favor with the landlord. God's hand was in everything, and He gave me the desires of my heart.

There are times you must keep pressing and not give up, even when everything seems to be going wrong. Keep pressing and believing. I am a witness to say that when things are going wrong, don't stop. Decree and declare out loud. Get into position and talk to Jesus. Tell Him that which is in your heart. Be honest and real. Our God is not dead; He is alive. He has always been on time, when I thought it was over and there was nothing more that I could do. Every time, God has been faithful to deliver me and show me that He has not forgotten me. Neither has our heavenly Father forgotten you. You belong to Him. Jeremiah 1:5 says, "Before I formed thee in the belly I knew thee; and before thou camest forth out of the womb I sanctified thee, and I ordained thee a prophet unto the nations." Imagine that! God had a purpose for you before you were even born.

For we are God's workmanship, created in Christ Jesus to do good works, which God prepared in advance for us to do. (Eph. 2:10)

According as he hath chosen us in him before the foundation of the world, that we should be holy and without blame before him in love. (Eph. 1:4)

Let God arise in your life, and let your enemies be

scattered. Allow Him to work on your behalf. You are about to experience something new and wonderful in your life, if you remain consistent in praying. Do not faint, and make a joyful noise unto the Lord (Ps. 100). Praise Him even when you do not feel like praising. You are strong in the name of Jesus. Plead the blood of Jesus Christ over your life, marriage, family, business and every area of your life. There is power in the blood. Decree and declare; do not be a bench warmer. Be on fire for Christ. You can do it! Let the fire of God fill you up and be with you every day. I pray the Spirit of the Lord will come upon you. Yes, the Spirit of the Lord God is very real!

It is time for new ideas, new visions to be led by the Spirit and not by the flesh. Everything that you say and do will be of God. I have met many people and divine connections that I would have never met on my own, if it had not been for prayer.

I will share a final testimony to encourage you. I was a single parent working as a care manager in a residential home. A week before Christmas, I knew that after paying rent and bills, there was very little left to buy food, not to mention Christmas presents for the children. I was living in a different city from my family, and I could not depend on them for support. I prayed, and one day after leaving work, I was a bit discouraged. I walked into the bank, knowing that I did not have much to work with. I was planning in my mind what was priority: food. I had to get a turkey and forget about the luxury of a Christmas cake and all the Christmas goodies that we usually took pleasure in having at Christmas.

I got to the bank teller, took care of the usual

business, and reluctantly asked for the balance. While holding the paper in my hand and not wanting to look at the amount, I decided to quickly glance at the balance. As I walked away, I stopped quite suddenly in shock. "Oh, no! Something is wrong." I rushed back to the banker.

She looked at me, puzzled, and asked, "Is there something wrong?" I asked her to check my, balance I was convinced something was wrong with the amount: there was way too much in my account. I needed to find out where all this money had come from. I had been praying, but when the money showed up in my account, I was shocked. I had the banker check and recheck, but she could not find where the money had come from—but it was mine!

I paused. "Okay, Lord." By this time, I was walking out of the bank, smiling and saying, "Thank You,

Jesus! Thank You." I had enough to buy food, all the goodies we loved at Christmas, and presents for my children. As I went into the meat shop to get my turkey, I was so excited.

But the Lord said clearly, "Do not buy the turkey."

I hesitated. "God, I need a turkey."

He said, "No, leave it."

I bought everything I needed, puzzled and a little disappointed about not having a turkey. However, I was very happy that I had more than enough. My children and I were going to have an awesome Christmas. When I arrived home, I praised God as I looked at all the shopping bags.

Before I could sit down, a dear church sister was at the front door with a smile on her face. She said, "The Lord told me to give this to you." In her hand was a large turkey. God did not stop there. She went out to her car and returned with a Christmas cake! I was praising God. The Word says, "I have not seen the righteous forsaken or his seed begging bread" (Ps. 37:35). God provided a supernatural money transfer into my account so that I was able to buy food, presents, and clothes. He sent the cake and turkey. There was nothing that I needed. God supplied all my needs.

I have prayed, and God has never failed me. I have prayed Psalm 23, 27, 35, 70, 91, and 121. I pray the Word over and over. Do not miss out on your blessing because you have been too distracted doing the wrong thing. God is going to use the remnant, those who have been positioning themselves in prayer. Revival is about to break out all over the world. People of God, "Present your bodies as a living sacrifice unto the Lord holy and acceptable which is your reasonable service. Do not be conformed to this world" (Rom. 12:1–2).

You Have the Keys—
Use Them

During a time of fasting and praying, the Lord gave me this word: "When you have been given the keys, you need to use it and not abuse it, in the name of Jesus. You have the authority to decree and declare, and to open the door to all areas of your life. The power is within you. You can do all that the Word says for you to do, and nothing is impossible with God. Open up your mouth and allow Jesus Christ to take every word and make it come to life. Make it happen in the name of Jesus."

He saith unto them, But whom say ye that I am? And Simon Peter answered and said, Thou art the Christ, the Son of the living God. And Jesus answered and said unto him, Blessed art thou, Simon Barjona: for flesh and blood hath not revealed it unto thee, but my Father which is in heaven. And I say also unto thee, That thou art Peter, and upon this rock I will build my church; and the gates of hell shall not prevail against it. And I will give unto thee the keys of the kingdom of heaven: and whatsoever thou shalt bind on earth shall be bound in heaven: and whatsoever thou shalt loose on earth shall be loosed

in heaven. (Matt. 16:15–19)

After receiving the word as I sat at my computer, I
wrote this poem.

Notes

You Have the Keys

Don't lose it—use it.

The power is in you.

Use it. Don't refuse it.

What you speak, it shall be.

Doors of opportunity will be open;

Favor will be upon your life.

Blessings will overflow you;

What you command, it shall be.

What you decree and declare

Will come forth.

Your life will change.

Let the words of your mouth

And the meditation

Of your heart be one of power.

Use it and unlock

All that has been given.

There are no limits.

You need to understand

Your future waits

For you to take a stand.

Use the keys that

Are in your hand.

Father, in the name of Jesus, I come into your presence, believing that you are Alpha and Omega, the beginning and the end. This is a new season. I decree and declare an open door is set before me, and no man will shut it. I decree and declare an open heaven over my life. I command every barrier and blockage to be removed now, in the name of Jesus. I command that the gates of hell shall not prevail against me, in Jesus's name. Every curse, spell, and witchcraft is broken now; I will not be denied what the Lord has for me. Help me, Lord, to do great exploits in the name of Jesus. All that You have for me will come forth in the name of Jesus. I will achieve. It is written that whatever things I ask for when I pray, I believe by faith I shall receive. In Jesus's name, amen.

Printed in the United States
By Bookmasters